creatures of the sea

Jellyfish

Other titles in the series:

creatures of the sea

Jellyfish

Kris Hirschmann

KIDHAVEN PRESS
An imprint of Thomson Gale, a part of The Thomson Corporation

THOMSON
GALE

Detroit • New York • San Francisco • San Diego • New Haven, Conn. • Waterville, Maine • London • Munich

© 2005 Thomson Gale, a part of The Thomson Corporation.

Thomson, Star Logo and KidHaven Press are trademarks and Gale is a registered trademark used herein under license.

For more information, contact
KidHaven Press
27500 Drake Rd.
Farmington Hills, MI 48331–3535
Or you can visit our Internet site at http://www.gale.com

LIBRARY OF CONGRESS CATALOGING–IN–PUBLICATION DATA

Hirschmann, Kris, 1967–
 Jellyfish / By Kris Hirschmann.
  p. cm. — (Creatures of the sea)
Summary: Discusses jellyfish anatomy, life cycle, habitat, and hunting methods.
Also discusses animals that appear to be jellyfish but are not.
Includes bibliographical references and index.
 ISBN 0–7377–2342–4 (hardback : alk. paper)
1. Jellyfishes—Juvenile literature. I.Title.
 QL377.S457 2004
 593.5'3—dc22

                                            2004007902

Printed in the United States of America

Table of contents

introduction

Fragile . . . but Tough

It is easy to see where jellyfish (sometimes called "jellies") get their name. These animals are soft all over, with no bones or shell. In the sea, a jelly's body gets all the support it needs from the surrounding water. In the open air, however, a jellyfish's body collapses into a pile of rubbery goop. A jelly that loses its watery support for even a moment is so badly damaged that it will soon die, even if it is immediately returned to the ocean.

It seems incredible that such a fragile animal can survive for long. But jellies do more than survive. In fact, they actually thrive in the world's oceans. These creatures can be found everywhere in the world—and at certain times of the year, enormous

With its soft body, a jellyfish swimming through the water looks like a very fragile animal.

numbers of them appear all at once. Some of these gatherings occur when water currents or winds push all of a region's jellies into one small area. Others happen when many jellies in one area grow to their adult size at the same time. In either of these situations, the water can become clogged with jellyfish.

These population explosions are unusual at a time when many sea creatures are in trouble. Their numbers are falling because of pollution, overfishing, and other human influences. But human activities do not appear to be any problem for jellyfish. These animals are just as plentiful as ever. In fact, some scientists think jellyfish populations may actually be growing. Few people fish for jellies, so overfishing is not an issue for these creatures. Jellies also have a much higher tolerance for pollution than most animals do. Sometimes they even move into areas that have been abandoned by other sea creatures, turning polluted regions into jellyfish "hot spots."

Today's ocean population trends prove that jellyfish can adapt to their surroundings and even shape them when conditions are right. This ability has helped jellies of all types to thrive in the world's oceans for millions of years. Some of the simplest creatures, it seems, are also the most successful.

Jelly Basics

Despite their name, jellyfish are not fish. They are **invertebrates,** or creatures without backbones. The invertebrate family is huge and includes insects, spiders, worms, shellfish, and many other animals. Jellyfish and their closest relatives—corals, sea anemones, and hydras—make up just one small part of the invertebrate family.

Several groups of sea creatures look like jellyfish. Only one of these groups, however, contains actual jellies. Scientists call these animals the "true jellyfish" to separate them from look-alike species. There are about two hundred species of true jellyfish.

Where Jellies Live

A few types of jellyfish live in saltwater lakes, but most jellies live in oceans and seas. These animals can be found in every ocean in the world, from the

After a storm, jellyfish like this one often wash up onto beaches where they dry out and die in the sun.

warm waters near the equator to the freezing seas near the earth's poles. Common warm-water species include the upside-down jellyfish (*Cassiopeia*), spotted jellies, and blue jellies. Cold-water species include the duncecap jellyfish, Arctic and Antarctic jellies, and many others.

Jellyfish are found not only in every ocean, they are found in every region of every ocean. These animals are equally common near land or out at sea. They often gather near beaches, where they bump into human swimmers. Evidence of these rubbery visitors can be seen after a storm, when thousands of jelly blobs wash up on the seashore and dry and die in the sun.

Most jellies float in the sunny upper layer of the sea. A few types, however, are found only miles below the ocean's surface. Some jellyfish even travel back and forth between shallow and deep environments. During the daytime, these jellies rise to the sea surface. At night, they sink deeper into the water.

The Jelly Body

All jellyfish share certain features, including general body arrangement. Jellyfish have **radial symmetry,** which means that their body parts spread out from a central point. In other words, a jellyfish has a top and bottom, but no front and back. If a person looked at a jellyfish from the side while it spun

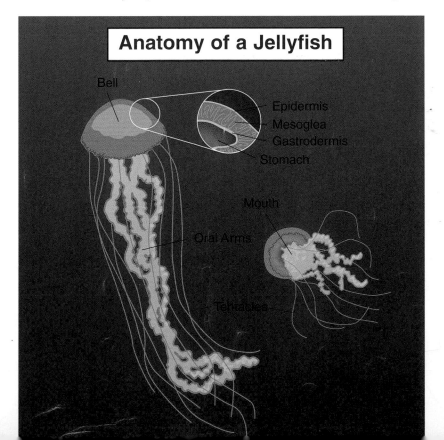

Anatomy of a Jellyfish

Bell

Epidermis

Mesoglea

Gastrodermis

Stomach

Mouth

Oral Arms

Tentacles

around on its central point, the jellyfish would look exactly the same all the way around.

The top part of a jellyfish is called the **bell.** Sometimes the bell is called the "umbrella" or "hood." The shape of this body part varies from species to species. Some jellyfish have circular, flattened bells. Others have cube-shaped, oval, or nearly round bells. In all species, the bell is covered by a thin skin called the **epidermis,** and the jelly's mouth and stomach are lined by another thin skin called the **gastrodermis.** The area between the epidermis and the gastrodermis is filled with a thick substance called the **mesoglea.** In many species, the mesoglea gives the jellyfish most of its shape and weight.

Attached around a jellyfish's mouth at the bottom center of the bell are flexible limbs called **oral arms.** Depending on the species, the oral arms may be short or long, thick or thin. Most jellyfish have four oral arms, but a few species have eight.

Thin strands called **tentacles** hang around the outer edge of the bottom of the bell like a fringe. Like the oral arms, these strands come in many different shapes and sizes. The number of tentacles also varies from species to species. Some jellyfish have just a few tentacles, while others have hundreds.

Identifying Jellyfish

Although jellyfish share many similarities, they also show some differences. One of the differences is

Arctic lion's mane jellyfish like these have a large bell and very long tentacles.

size. Some jellyfish are enormous. The bell of the Arctic lion's mane jellyfish, for example, can measure more than seven feet (2.1 meters) across. This creature's longest tentacles can be 120 feet (36.6 meters) long. Most jellyfish, however, are much smaller than this, measuring from a few inches to a foot from one side of the bell to the other. Several species are only about one inch across. These size differences help scientists to identify jellyfish species.

Color is another way to tell jellyfish apart. Some jellies are completely transparent, or see-through. Others are mostly transparent but have solid-colored internal organs. These organs are visible right through the jellies' bodies. Still other species may be white, brown, blue, smoky, or other colors. Some jellyfish also bear spots or stripes. Colors and patterns are important clues to a jelly's identity.

On the Move

All jellyfish, regardless of size, shape, or color, seem to pulsate, or pump in rhythm, as they drift through their ocean homes. This pulsation is the jelly's way of swimming. A jellyfish lets its bell open wide and fill with water. It then uses muscles attached to the bottom surface of the bell and the mesoglea to pull inward. This pull makes the bell get smaller. As it shrinks, water is pumped out of the bell. This

The internal organs of this jellyfish can be seen through its transparent body.

creates a push that forces the jelly forward or upward, depending on which way its bell is pointing.
The push may be gentle, hard, smooth, or jerky,
depending on the species.

Jellies swim very slowly. Even the biggest jelly
travels just a couple of feet with each push, and
small jellies can only produce a tiny squirt of power
when they squeeze their bells. So swimming is not
a good way for a jelly to travel very far. Jellies swim
mostly to maintain position or to move up or
down. For long-distance travel, jellies depend on
water currents to move them around. Still, swimming is very important to a jellyfish—so important,
in fact, that it is controlled by "pacemaker" nerves
in the jelly's body. These nerves send out regular
signals that force the jellyfish to squeeze and release,
squeeze and release in rhythm, just like nerves in
the human body keep the heart beating at all times.

Senses at Work

The jellyfish's pacemaker nerves are part of a network just beneath the epidermis. This nerve network serves as the jellyfish's brain. It spreads
throughout the body and controls all of the jellyfish's actions.

The nerve network also controls the jellyfish's
senses. A jellyfish can use light receptors, or sensors,
around the edge of its bell to tell the difference between light and dark. The edge of the bell also has

A colorful jelly with long tentacles squeezes its bell in order to push itself upward.

balance receptors that help the jellyfish stay upright in the water. Smell receptors pick up and identify chemicals in the water. And touch receptors in the tentacles and mouth tell the jellyfish when it bumps into something.

Jellyfish are very simple animals, so none of these senses is well developed. A jellyfish cannot understand or respond to its surroundings in the same way a more advanced animal might. But a jelly knows enough. These creatures have drifted in the world's oceans for more than 500 million years, so it is obvious that they have the tools they need to survive.

chapter

2

Life Cycle
of the Jellyfish

An adult jellyfish is properly called a **medusa**.
(The plural of medusa is medusae.) The medusa
is the jellyfish's final, largest, free-swimming form,
and it is the one with which most people are famil-
iar. But jellyfish are medusae for only a short part of
their lives. These animals have complicated life cy-
cles that include several different body shapes and
some dramatic changes.

Starting Out
The jellyfish life cycle starts with the medusa par-
ents. These adult jellies are either male or female.
Both sexes have reproductive organs called **gonads**
inside their bodies. Inside the gonads, males make
sperm and females make eggs. The sperm or eggs

The jellyfish spends only a very short part of its life cycle as an adult, when it is known as a medusa.

pass into the jellyfish's stomach. After that, a male jelly spits his sperm out of his mouth, which opens at the bottom center of the bell. Where a female jelly's eggs go next depends on her species.

Once the eggs and sperm are created, they must meet. This meeting happens in different ways for different jellyfish species. In some species, eggs get stuck to frilly edges around the female's mouth after they leave her stomach. When the female swims through a patch of water containing a male's sperm, the eggs and sperm bump together. In other species, the female holds her eggs inside her stomach. The male's sperm swim right through the female's mouth and into her stomach, where they fertilize the waiting eggs. The fertilized eggs then leave the mouth and enter special holes in the female's oral arms. They stay in the arms while they develop.

It is likely that other species leave the fertilization process completely to chance. Both eggs and sperm are released into the water, where they float freely. If the eggs and sperm meet, fertilization will occur. If they do not, the eggs will not be fertilized, and they will never develop. Jellyfish increase their chances of fertilization by releasing millions of eggs and sperm. When such huge numbers are involved, some eggs and sperm are bound to meet.

The Planula Phase

Fertilized eggs develop for a short time before hatching. The animal that emerges from the egg is called a **planula**. (The plural of planula is planulae.) A planula looks nothing like an adult jellyfish. A planula is flat and oval, and the edge of its body is lined with delicate hairs called **cilia.** The cilia beat to push the planula through the water. Helped by ocean currents, the planula swims away from the area where it hatched.

At this point the planula usually joins the plankton, which is a floating population of tiny plants and creatures near the sea surface. If the planula is lucky, it will not be eaten by any of the other little creatures in the plankton. It floats for a short time

—just a few hours or days. Then the planula leaves the plankton and swims toward the ocean floor. It settles onto a solid surface such as a rock and gives off a sticky substance to glue itself firmly to it. The little creature is now ready to enter the next phase of its life.

The Polyp Phase

Once the planula attaches itself to a solid surface on the ocean floor, it starts to grow and change. Soon it turns into a creature called a **polyp.** The polyp looks like a tube with a fringe around the top edge. In the middle of the fringe is the polyp's mouth.

The baby jellyfish seen on the polyp on the left are nearly ready to break away and become medusae.

At this point the polyp is tiny—too small for people to see without magnification. Its mouth is also minuscule, measuring just .004 of an inch (0.1 millimeter) across. As tiny as it is, however, the polyp is able to eat even smaller animals. The polyp sucks in any food it can catch. Over time it grows bigger and stronger. Little buds also begin growing from the polyp's tubelike trunk. When these buds reach a certain size, they drop off the polyp and glue themselves to a hard surface on the sea floor. Then they, too, become polyps. Eventually, a whole colony of polyps springs up around the original animal. A single fertilized egg has now turned into dozens or even hundreds of creatures.

New Jellyfish

The polyps may grow for a couple of years. When they get big enough, their bodies begin to change again. The tube part of each polyp's body develops horizontal grooves. These grooves get deeper and deeper until the polyp looks like a stack of fringed dinner plates. The upper plates develop more quickly than the lower ones. As each top plate matures, it breaks away from the polyp and drifts off in the ocean currents. One by one the lower plates also mature and break away.

The floating polyp parts are not really plates, of course. They are baby jellyfish. The little jellies eat and grow, eat and grow. They get bigger very quickly.

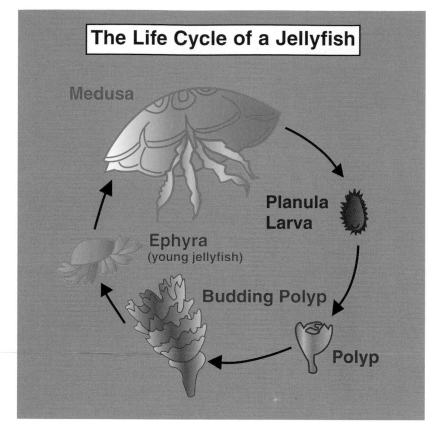

The Life Cycle of a Jellyfish

Medusa

Planula Larva

Ephyra
(young jellyfish)

Budding Polyp

Polyp

It takes just a few weeks for the jellyfish to take on their adult shapes and colors. At this point the animals are still small, but they are definitely medusae.

A jellyfish that reaches the medusa stage is nearing the end of its life. In most species it takes just a few months for a fledgling medusa to reach its adult size and release eggs or sperm into the water. The medusa dies after this task is complete.

Out of Nowhere

When water conditions are right, all of an area's polyps may mature around the same time. The polyps shed tiny medusae into the water by the millions. At first, the new jellies are so small that they can barely be seen, but the little creatures grow quickly. Before long, the jellyfish are big and their populations may be huge, stretching over thousands of square miles of ocean. These jellyfish **blooms,** as they are often called, seem to come out of nowhere. They may last for a few months before currents and winds carry the jellies away or dump them in smelly, decaying piles on nearby seashores.

It seems like a sad end for the jellyfish. But from nature's point of view, the goal has been accomplished. The jellyfish medusae have lived long enough to produce eggs and sperm. By the time a bloom dies off, a new generation of planulae has hatched and settled to the ocean floor. Over time the planulae will change into polyps, and then medusae, continuing the jelly cycle of life.

Eat to Survive

Jellyfish are **predators,** which means they hunt other animals for food. Jellies eat mostly **zooplankton,** or the tiny animals within the plankton layer. However, jellyfish will eat almost anything they can catch, including fish, small crustaceans (animals with external shells, such as shrimp and krill), and even other jellies.

Catching these animals is mostly a matter of luck. Jellyfish are not active hunters. They simply drift along and bump into their prey. Fortunately for jellies, the oceans are a virtual soup of tiny creatures. Just by floating in the water, a jellyfish is almost sure to catch all the food it needs to survive.

Catching Prey

Tentacles are the jellyfish's main hunting tools. In many species, the tentacles trail behind the body like long fishing lines. In other species, the tentacles form a short fringe around the bell. Whether long or short, the tentacles are usually transparent, making them nearly impossible to see. Small animals brush against the tentacles without realizing they are there.

For the prey, this is a deadly mistake. A jellyfish's tentacles are lined with thousands of stinging cells called **nematocysts.** Each nematocyst contains a hollow, coiled thread with a sharp barb on the end. Even the lightest touch triggers the nematocysts,

A fish caught in the tentacles of a jellyfish is paralyzed by the venom in the jelly's stinging cells.

which then shoot their barbs into the prey's flesh. Soon the jelly and its prey are connected by thousands of tiny strands. The jelly then pumps venom into its prey through the hollow threads and barbs. The venom quickly paralyzes the prey. Because the helpless animal can no longer struggle or fight, there is no chance that it will damage the jelly's fragile body as the jelly eats it.

Jellyfish never run out of nematocysts. As soon as one of these cells fires, a new cell begins to grow in its place. This means that jellyfish are always ready to capture food, whenever and wherever a meal may appear.

Eating and Digestion

Once prey has been caught, it is time for the jellyfish to eat. A jelly uses its oral arms to pull food from the tentacles. The oral arms then carry the food to the jellyfish's mouth and stuff it inside. The jellyfish does not chew its prey in any way. It immediately passes the food through its mouth and into its stomach. In transparent species, it is possible to see the jellyfish's meal right through the walls of the bell.

In the stomach, the digestion process begins. Because undigested food is heavy and slows the jellyfish down, the stomach works quickly to dissolve its meal. The jelly's body absorbs the nutrients in its prey. Then it ejects shells and whatever else cannot

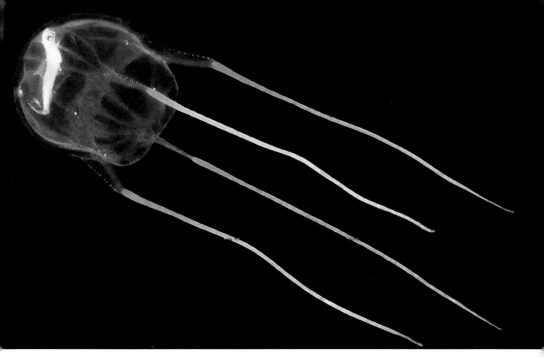

A partially digested fish can be seen in the bell of this box jellyfish.

be digested. The mouth is the only way into or out of a jellyfish, so waste products go back out the same way they came in.

A jellyfish's body is made almost entirely of water. Flesh makes up just 5 percent of a jelly's weight. For this reason, jellyfish do not need to eat much to survive. They can get by with very little food for long periods and can even shrink to save energy when necessary. When food is plentiful, however, jellyfish grow extremely quickly. Since jellies usually drift through food-rich areas, fast growth is common for these creatures.

Unusual Eaters

Although most jellies use the sting-and-paralyze method to catch food, some do not. Some species shoot sticky threads from their nematocysts rather than barbed ones. The sticky threads glue themselves to the prey's flesh instead of poking through it. Other species shoot very long threads that wrap themselves around the prey's body. The entangled prey is then brought to the jelly's mouth.

Some jellyfish do not use nematocysts at all. Instead, they have sticky bodies that snag any prey the jellies happen to bump into. Hairs on the jellyfish's body then push the prey toward the mouth. And

Rhizostomes like this jellyfish have hundreds of little mouths lined with cilia that drag tiny animals into the jelly's body.

jellies called rhizostomes have hundreds or even thousands of little mouths instead of one big one. The oral arms are dotted with these little mouths, and each little mouth is lined with cilia. The cilia beat constantly to create currents that drag microscopic animals into the jelly's body.

Eating Algae

A few types of jellyfish do not have to hunt at all. These animals grow their own food inside their bodies! To get the process started, a young jellyfish swallows a mass of algae, a kind of plant. Instead of digesting the algae, however, the jelly passes them into the flesh of its bell. There the algae live and reproduce. As they do, they release sugars and chemicals as waste products. These waste products are absorbed by the jellyfish, which uses them as an energy source. In return for this favor, the jellyfish helps the algae by spending lots of time in the sun each day. Sunlight passes through the jelly's transparent body and gives the algae the energy they need to survive.

One of the world's best-known populations of algae-eating jellyfish lives in the saltwater lakes of Palau, an island nation in the Pacific Ocean. Huge swarms of softball-sized jellies crowd together in the sunny parts of these lakes. As the sun shifts position in the sky throughout the day, the jellyfish also shift to keep themselves—and their algae—directly in the sun's rays.

Jelly Defenses

Jellyfish are predators, but they are also eaten by sea turtles, birds, ocean sunfish, and many other creatures. With their soft bodies and slow movements, jellies cannot fight or flee when a predator approaches. Nonetheless, they do have a few ways to protect themselves.

The nematocysts are the jelly's most important defense. Unlike smaller creatures, larger animals are not usually paralyzed by the jellyfish's sting. Still, the sting hurts. For this reason many animals will not eat jellyfish, no matter how hungry they are. Even a dead jellyfish is not safe to eat. Because

A sea turtle feeds on a moon jellyfish. Because they are slow swimmers and have soft bodies, jellyfish are easy prey.

The Australian box jelly's poisonous tentacles can kill a human in just a few minutes.

nematocysts fire automatically, a long-dead pile of goo on a beach can deliver a sting just like a living jellyfish can.

A few jellyfish have unusually powerful stings. A touch from these animals can bring agonizing pain, sickness, and even death to any creature foolish enough to approach. One especially dangerous species is the Australian box jelly, also called the sea wasp. The sea wasp may be the world's most venomous animal. Humans who get wrapped up in this creature's tentacles sometimes die within a few minutes. Other dangerous species include the enormous Arctic lion's mane jellyfish and the tiny irukandji jelly.

Another unusual jellyfish defense is called **bioluminescence.** Bioluminescence is natural light produced by a living creature. Many jellies can flash blue or green lights inside their bodies when they are threatened. Some scientists think that jellyfish use these lights to startle predators and, if all goes well, to scare them away.

The easiest way for a jellyfish to stay safe, of course, is to avoid being seen in the first place. So for many jellies, transparency is the best defense. A clear jellyfish drifts quietly through its underwater world, attracting little attention to itself. If the jelly is lucky, it will not run into any hungry predators. It will have a full life of hunting and eating and will grow into the full-sized adult it was meant to be.

Jellyfish Impostors

The oceans are full of jellyfish impostors. In many ways, these species look and act like jellyfish—but they are not. Differences in the ways these creatures develop, move, eat, and more set them apart from the true jellies.

The Hydrozoans

A family of animals called the **hydrozoans** contains the creatures most often mistaken for jellyfish. There are about ten thousand hydrozoan species. Most of these species look nothing like jellyfish. Some hydrozoans, for instance, group together in coral-like colonies. Others never develop beyond the polyp stage. Still others become adults so tiny that they would never be mistaken for their jelly relatives.

A few hydrozoans, however, grow into free-swimming adults that are big enough to resemble true jellies. The largest hydrozoans can grow to about six inches (152.4 millimeters) across. Hydrozoan jellies of all sizes are usually transparent, and many are bioluminescent. They look almost exactly like true jellyfish, but a thin shelf of skin around the bottom inner edge of the bell gives these creatures away. This shelf, called the **velum,** is not present in the true jellies.

Habitat is another way to identify hydrozoan jellies. True jellyfish never live in freshwater, but hydrozoans sometimes do. The most common freshwater

Although the Portuguese man o' war looks like a jelly, it belongs to a family of animals called the hydrozoans.

hydrozoan, *Craspedacusta,* can be found in lakes and rivers throughout the United States. These animals tend to be small, measuring just one-quarter inch to one inch (6.4 to 25.4 millimeters) across. They usually appear in late August or early September, when the water is warm and food is plentiful. *Craspedacusta* has stinging cells that it uses to capture prey, but it is not dangerous to people. This creature's tiny barbs are not strong enough to penetrate human skin.

Portuguese Man o' War

Perhaps the best-known hydrozoan is the Portuguese man o' war. This animal can be found all over the world, wherever tropical ocean currents flow.

Unlike most jellyfish, the Portuguese man o' war does not float unseen within the ocean. Instead, the top part of this creature's body is a sort of gas-filled balloon that bobs on the water's surface. The balloon can be up to sixteen inches (406.4 millimeters) long, and it is usually bright blue. It has flattened edges that act like boat sails to catch ocean breezes. The man o' war can raise or lower its balloon "crest" to change the way it catches the wind, thereby changing its speed or direction as well.

Trailing below the balloon are many tentacles. Some of the tentacles are short, but others are very long. The longest man o' war tentacles can stretch more than 150 feet (45.7 meters) behind the balloon. These tentacles are equipped with thousands

The tentacles on this Portuguese man o' war have thousands of nematocysts containing deadly venom.

of nematocysts that fire barbed threads when touched. Once embedded in the skin of prey, the barbs release a venom nearly as strong as that of a cobra. The venom can kill a human if enough barbs pierce the skin. Fewer stings do not kill, but they cause intense pain and red "whip marks" that remain visible on the skin for months.

Because the man o' war's tentacles can grow so long, it is not safe to enter the water when these animals are anywhere within view. People who live in man o' war-infested areas try very hard to avoid these beautiful but dangerous creatures.

Comb Jellies

Another family of animals often mistaken for jellyfish is the comb jellies, or **ctenophores.** There are between 100 and 150 different types of comb jellies. All of these animals have jellylike, transparent bodies. Many comb jellies float in the ocean's surface waters, like true jellyfish, and many also trail long tentacles behind their bodies. Some even pulse their bodies to swim, like the true jellies do. With so many similarities, it is easy to see why these animals are considered jellyfish by people around the world.

But there are many important differences between comb jellies and true jellies. One major difference involves the way these animals move through the water. Comb jellies—even the pulsating ones—

Transparent comb jellies, another jellyfish impostor, make a tasty meal for these bright orange cup corals.

do not squeeze water out of their bodies to push themselves forward. Instead, their bodies are lined with eight rows of cilia. The cilia beat together like miniature oars to move the comb jelly through the water. The beating cilia also cause an interesting effect. They scatter light rays in a way that makes parts of the comb jelly seem to glow. This false glow can be almost any color and is a good way to identify comb jellies.

The ability to sting is another difference between comb jellies and true jellyfish. Although some comb jellies have tentacles, no comb jellies have stinging cells. One type of comb jelly, called *Haeckelia,* fakes this ability by eating jellyfish, saving the nematocysts, and storing them in its tentacles. When touched, the stored nematocysts fire just as they would have in their original jellyfish home. Once the barbs discharge, however, the nematocysts cannot grow back. The *Haeckelia* must find and eat more jellyfish to replace its lost weapons.

Comb Jelly Invasion

The most interesting comb jelly story comes from the Black Sea. In the early 1980s, a group of comb jellies nicknamed the sea walnuts was accidentally

The rows of beating cilia that line the body of this comb jelly make it seem to glow.

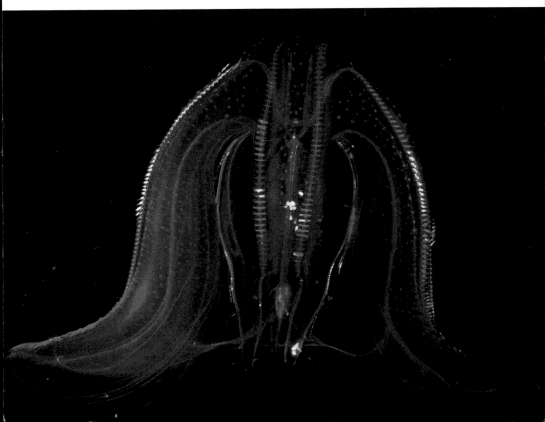

released into this body of water. These ctenophores were smaller than a human thumb, but they were fierce and hungry predators. They gobbled down every tiny creature they could find. Because the Black Sea did not contain any predators that eat comb jellies, the population of these little animals exploded. Within a few years the jellies were swarming everywhere. Meanwhile, native fish and other animals starved to death as the hungry jellies ate their food.

A few years later, another ctenophore called the oval comb jelly accidentally reached the Black Sea. Comb jellies eat each other, and the oval comb jellies are currently feasting on the sea walnuts. This situation is reducing the sea walnut population, which is good. The oval jelly population, however, is getting bigger and bigger. In the end, it does not really matter which jelly wins this war. The Black Sea will still be jammed with ctenophores that were never meant to be there in the first place.

This story, however, proves an important point. Like all creatures, jellyfish and their relatives must be able to adjust to changing situations. Comb jellies, hydrozoans, and true jellies may be blob-shaped, spineless, and brainless—but they are far from helpless. These simple creatures are showing today, as they have for millions of years, that they are perfectly equipped to survive in the harsh ocean world.

Glossary

bell: The main, usually rounded, top part of a jellyfish's body.

bioluminescence: Natural light created within the body of a living creature.

blooms: Sudden surges in jellyfish populations.

cilia: Tiny hairs that beat rhythmically to create currents.

ctenophores: Comb jellies. Often mistaken for true jellyfish.

epidermis: The thin upper layer of skin of the bell.

gastrodermis: The thin lower layer of skin of the bell.

gonads: Organs inside a jellyfish that make eggs or sperm.

hydrozoans: Close relatives of the true jellyfish that are often mistaken for jellyfish.

invertebrates: Creatures without backbones.

medusa: The adult, free-swimming form of a jellyfish.

mesoglea: A jellylike substance between the epidermis and the gastrodermis.

nematocysts: The stinging cells on the tentacles of the jellyfish.

oral arms: Four to eight arms that hang around a jellyfish's mouth.

planula: A newly hatched jellyfish.

polyp: Phase of the jellyfish life cycle when it is attached to a solid surface.

predator: Any animal that hunts other animals to survive.

radial symmetry: Even arrangement around a central point.

tentacles: Thin strands that hang from the outer edge of the bell.

velum: A skin shelf around the bottom inner edge of an adult hydrozoan's bell.

zooplankton: Tiny animals that live in the plankton layer.

For Further Exploration

Books

Mary M. Cerullo, *The Truth About Dangerous Sea Creatures*. San Francisco: Chronicle, 2003. This book looks at a variety of dangerous sea creatures. Venomous jellyfish, as well as sharks, squids, octopuses, and other animals, are discussed.

Morris K. Jacobson and David R. Franz, *Wonders of Jellyfish*. New York: Dodd, Mead, 1978. This book is a deeper examination of jellyfish in general. It spotlights some especially interesting species.

Sharon Sharth, *Sea Jellies: From Corals to Jellyfish*. New York: Franklin Watts, 2002. Read about jellyfish and their relatives in this informative book.

Periodical

William M. Hamner, "Australia's Box Jellyfish: A Killer Down Under," *National Geographic*, August 1994. This article profiles the world's most venomous creature.

Web Sites

The JelliesZone (www.jellieszone.com). This site includes sections about jellies in the news, jellyfish photography, and much more. It also features a good page of frequently asked questions.

Jellyfish (www.enchantedlearning.com/subjects/ invertebrates/jellyfish/Jellyfishcoloring.shtml). This page includes some basic jellyfish information plus a life-cycle diagram to print out and color.

index

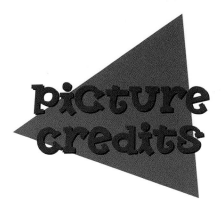

picture credits

Cover image: Photos.com

© Brandon D. Cole/CORBIS, 25

Jenny and Tony Enderby/Lonely Planet Images, 34

Chris Jouan, 11

© Doug Perrine/SeaPics.com, 30

Photos.com, 7, 14, 16, 18, 36, 39

Franco Silvi/EPA/Landov, 10

Karen Trist/Lonely Planet Images, 31

© Masa Ushioda/SeaPics.com, 27

Ingo Wagner/DPA/Landov, 13

Mark Webster/Lonely Planet Images, 28

© Stuart Westmorland/CORBIS, 38

© 2004 David Wrobel/SeaPics.com, 20

about the author

Kris Hirschmann has written more than one hundred books for children. She is the president of The Wordshop, a business that provides a variety of writing and editorial services. She holds a bachelor's degree in psychology from Dartmouth College in Hanover, New Hampshire. Hirschmann lives just outside Orlando, Florida, with her husband, Michael, and her daughters, Nikki and Erika.